# We Are Beautiful Like Snowflakes

*poems by*

# Lisa Rhodes-Ryabchich

*Finishing Line Press*
Georgetown, Kentucky

# We Are Beautiful
Like Snowflakes

Copyright © 2016 by Lisa Rhodes-Ryabchich
ISBN 978-1-63534-012-9 First Edition
All rights reserved under International and Pan-American Copyright Conventions. No part of this book may be reproduced in any manner whatsoever without written permission from the publisher, except in the case of brief quotations embodied in critical articles and reviews.

## ACKNOWLEDGMENTS

    I want to express my heartfelt gratitude and love to my parents Joel and Rosemarie Rhodes, my daughter Kyla Jolie Ryabchich, and my sister Leslie Ann Rhodes for their endless encouragement and support. A special thanks to Aunt Desiree and Aunt Shirley for their support. My warmest appreciation to Huihwah Jung, Yifan Sun, Richie Ramphal, June Francis Coleman, Douglas Brown, Shittu Fowora, Suzanne Cleary, Dan Masterson, Sherry Reiter, Nick Mazza, Tom Lux, Kevin Pilkington, Cornelius Eady, Pilar V. Arsenec, Denize Lauture, Suffern Poetry Slam, Cave Canem, Sarah Lawrence College, Susan Guma, Marilyn Nelson for her wonderful lecture on the importance of rhyme and meter, Myra Goldberg, Joan Silber, Jennifer Knox, Myronn Hardy, Jacqueline Jones LaMon, Alexander Weinstein, Yusef Komunyakaa, Tyehimba Jess , Christopher Cipro, Francine J Harris, Evie Schockley, Michael Affa Weaver, Jeffrey McDaniel, and Dante Micheaux. Thank you and God Bless you all for your kind words, encouragement and support of my poetry.
    Undying gratitude to Finishing Line Press at http://www.finishinglinepress.com
and their warm supportive staff Leah Maines, Christen Kincaid and Elizabeth Maines. Thank you for this privilege.
    Finally, grateful acknowledgement to Joshua Rebell and Cornelius Street Café where these poems were first heard.


Publisher: Leah Maines
Editor: Christen Kincaid
Cover Art: Miss Linda, Artistrising.com
Author Photo: Glamour Shots

Printed in the USA on acid-free paper.
Order online: www.finishinglinepress.com
            also available on amazon.com

Author inquiries and mail orders:
Finishing Line Press
P. O. Box 1626
Georgetown, Kentucky 40324
U. S. A.

# Table of Contents

The Apartment Hunt ............................................................. 1
Age ......................................................................................... 2
1940's Reprieve .................................................................... 3
Self-Respect Motto ............................................................. 5
Life upon a Dream .............................................................. 6
The Solace of the Social Worker ....................................... 7
Dishonesty ............................................................................ 8
A Love Letter ....................................................................... 9
Cat Fight ............................................................................. 10
We Are Beautiful Like Snowflakes ................................. 11
For the Unmarried Woman ............................................. 12
Adolescence ....................................................................... 14
The Question ..................................................................... 17
Dreaming of Seville, Spain .............................................. 18
The Healing ....................................................................... 20
Save the Good Children ................................................... 22
Grandma Rhodes Remembered From a Photo
    Taken in Florida ........................................................... 23
Unspoken Butterflies ........................................................ 27
I'd Like To .......................................................................... 28
Congolese Confidence ..................................................... 29
Self-Love ............................................................................ 30

*for my mother and father*

## The Apartment Hunt (1988)
*"Steal away, steal away, steal away to Jesus."*
—*African American spiritual*

We are looking at some
      apartments, Choosing which
Damaged pad, would Lend my
      time, House my ambitions—
A place to Fetch water,
      seize my Inhibitions!
I'm Black!—Imagine that!—
      No job—preconditions?
Just thrilled to live in a
      new Situation. Is
This desperation? This
      pad has Austerity—
I can't say *Grace* here, or
      take off my clothes here—Breathe
The fresh air. Stale odors
      In rooms, Made me recall
The *mounds* of People once
      Trapped, in this cell, Tearing
Apart all family roots.
      Look at me! Bent out of
Shape, And listening, for
      the ghosts of Black slaves,
Still frustrated, About
      being Locked-out, of a
Pad, Once again, that had
      no use for Them, and all
Their broken-hearted, Dreams.

# Age
### *for Sandra Blane*

What is age?—Tourniquet—
Clamping around my throat?

Each year drops of blood, pool
To a darker shade.

What is beginning *End?*
Is age beginning *End?*

If I lived other lives—
What provisions were set?

What is age?—Tourniquet—
Clamping around my throat?

Is it a scar of 2
Numerals—a red rule?

A calendar of activism,
From birth through decades
Of wars and racism?

What is age?—Tourniquet—
Clamping around my throat?

## 1940's Reprieve

Sometimes, I think I'm a lot
Like my father, and have lived
When he lived, when the streets were
Cobblestoned, and milk was 5-
Cents a bottle, and movies
Were, quality Hollywood
Pictures. A kiss was filled with
Passion, and everybody
Knew who Burt Lancaster was.
Good women smiled, with a
Cherry blossom, on their rosy
Cheeks, and a purple haze of
Roses, glowed in a halo
Around their heads. My mother
As a child, would have to
Rise from sleep, very early
And shovel coal, from beneath
The basement, in her home, to
Heat the building, her father
Leased. This laborious, odd job—
Tortured her. She had nightmares
And flashbacks, even after
She was married. But the child
Labor laws don't matter, when
You are poor. She was like, a
Little slave, while her father
Dished out, his brutal orders.
My father, took orders, in
The Marines, as a draftee.
He had to witness, the planes
Crash, in the Korean War,
And watch, a drill sergeant, rob
His team Comrades, in Boot Camp.

He luckily worked, for the
*Commanding Officer,* a
General, who let him use
His jeep service. He and mom
Married, at the *Altar* in
A famous Catholic Church
With a few hard earned dollars
In savings, and a lot of
Pride, and hope for the future.

**Self-Respect Motto**

I respect myself,
Because I am well-
Prepared! I honor
Myself, because I
Know, I do care! I
Carry myself, with
Pride and self-esteem!
I embellish my-
Self with positive
Thoughts! I teach myself—
I know how to learn!
I own myself! I
Accept my duties.
I nurture myself!
I deserve to give
And accept love! I
Have a strong backbone!

## Life upon a Dream

That *Pixie* sharp haircut,
Framed a little girl's face—
Her dark, mysterious
Eyes, watched across blessed
Lake's, yellow span. She wears
A dress—blue pressed, barely
Stands, with knobby-knees. Is
That me?—Wearing my dress
That I used to wear?—A
Little red dress, with white
Frill around the collar,
Except hers is blue? She looks
Like me—her spirit explodes,
As she rubs her charms, like
A shiny, new penny,
While she leans to, daring
Dock, next to a rowboat.
Row, row, row your boat, gently
Down the stream, merrily…
Merrily…Merrily…
        Is life upon a dream?

## The Solace of the Social Worker
*for Leslie Ann*

Sister's distinct presence, being
an attentive social worker,
working her world—arranging,
each of us like stairs on an arched
staircase—snuggly surrounding
us with friends, and relatives
once known. The day grew hotter
passersby passed. I noticed
an all-girl click carrying
schoolbooks composed. A sistas'
cautious brown eyes, drilled tightly
knitted rules, preaching the word
to the world outside, their stead.
My thoughts of social graces
reverberated, as she said:
"*Sistas*', don't break any rules—
don't embarrass me, but walk tall!
Be proud of the things you learned in school!"

**Dishonesty**

Lies, lies! Nothing but
A record of lies!
Left behind, despise
Watery eye's guise,
Sitting comforted,
Body positioned—
Stretched in curl, with feet
Lying on top, of
Each other, so warmth
Permeates electric
Body, plugged into
Lies, no better then
Sordid flies, cuddling
Their eggs—diseased spies
Infested, to contain
The well fertilized
Womb, moving pensively
Then retreating lies!
Stillness, heats the fuse—
Pulse black, pumps black smoke!

**A Love Letter**

I am the brightest ebb, of light,
That has entered into your sphere!
Please have no fear, because I am
Here, to salvage my kind life, in
The nights of inspiration, sent
From above. Each star, represents
The power, of love and knowledge.
They hold all my secrets. Pray on
All the stars, to guide you my way!
Maybe, there is a place in my
Heart, for you to stay, in spite of
Your inconstant feelings, that tend
To go astray! Perhaps, one day
We will meet, amidst the towers
Of light, sent, from another place
Far away? I beckon, for your
Love, and for all my endeavors
To be successful, in this good
Life. Hurry! Time, has a way, of
Running out. I hope, to send this
Letter, before the next moon, shines
On the radiant, black, passionate night!

**Cat Fight**
    *for Mittens (d. 2012)*


A black pretty, yellow-eyed cat, followed
My lead, inside the house, where I left him, diced
Food. I closed the door, quickly, behind him—
When he rushed for the food. At last! I roar,
I have got you this time, my fine, soft friend!
I locked him in, with Mister Mittens—
The King of Cats, living the grandest life.
They fought at first, spit, sputtered across, rife
Lips, clenching claws, raised a roar, until, I
Said, No more! No More!

## We Are Beautiful like Snowflakes
*for Kyla Jolie*

What a beautiful pink cloud, Floating by, high up in
The sky. Looks like Snow, for tomorrow... Let it snow
Let it snow... so we can fly high, free, in the Blue
Glorious sky, like a snowflake, so beautiful
Crystalline, a living Spirit, spreading vibrant
Energetic pulses, across the Universe
Like syncopated drops, of *Light bursts*—miracle
Powder, awakening the World, to a wondrous
Magical, new moment—another Glorious
World, all the way to a new dimension, of mother-
Human Spirit—a path across the skyway, ripples
Like a human heartbeat, keeping you *Alive*, with
The hands, of a great *God*, invisibly connected
To everything, and everyone, like the love, that gives
Birth, when a baby takes, her first Voice lesson, in
The delivery Room, and her face, wants an arm, to
Burrow into, and the Words, "I'm so happy to
See you," coming through her mother's Lips, smiling with
Ecstasy, saying: You are the first, and Last born—
The legacy of Us—the seed that will flourish
Beyond the walls, that don't Need to be here, and you
Will sour into flight, like a *New* star—a rare being—
An incredible Gift, you are every second, every day, flows
The rest, of your God-given, beautiful natural life!

## For the Unmarried Woman

When you wake-up
In the morning—
There is a hard
Notch to burn. A
Maze of wonder,
And loneliness
*Stigmata*, scars
On the shoulders.
The nights have been
Heated, with passion,
And sensuous, smells—
Enlightening
The imagination:
Juicy peaches,
Sweet green, grapes,
*Tropical Island-*
*Dark Coconut*
*Tanning Oil*, blew
Off the coast, embracing
You, in a heavenly
Cloud, of silk, and
Cinnamon-maple
Wisps. Was it so
Tantalizing
To your pores—breathing
Into the balmy
Blue, night sky, twinkling
With stars, and jets
Pacing overhead,
In zodiac-
Formation, waiting
Like dozens, of
Emerald gems,

Boasting, underneath
The ocean's sleek
Lining, deep near
The hell, where the
*Devil Fish* gather?

**Adolescence**

Do I think, these
Words, I speak? Do
I write, these
Words, that I write?
The inflection
Of your speech, has
A definite, octave
Pitch, that I don't
Have. Your intrusive
Personality,
Obstinately
Obstinates, my
Personality—
And tries to be
Present, even though
I don't need, or
Desire you, to
Be there. At times,
You hide me, with
Your presence, and
I protest, and abhor
You greatly! You
Bring others, to
Do the same, looking
At me strangely!
I feel subdued?
Annoyed?
Temporarily
And
Tempestuously—
I seek refuge,

In the clearing,
Overlooking
Dried-leaves, scattered
From old-age, hidden,
Among the rocks,
And twigs, nestling
Like padding, against
The barren earth.
Peace, was congruent,
With the little plants

Looming, far above
The tallest trees—
Stretching farther
And farther, showing
Me, their secrets
Of survival,
Amidst the woods.
The ferns, and neat
Rows, of pine trees
Watch, the staunch—
Valuable,
Decorative
Tiny plants, with
Hut-like domes, covering
Them for shelter—
Admiring,
Them, for their strong
Confidence, and
Perseverance.
I sense a glow
Of happiness,

As I watch, the
Sun, on a smooth
Round, white rock, like-
Alabaster,
Reflecting near-
By, the bushes'
Simplicity—
The clove-like leaves,
On this rock, of mirrors.

**The Question**

To be examined,
In a box,

Set on a table—
With your head

Split open—
An examiner

Examining, your
Organ's parts—

Taking apart, dead
Internal-mechanisms—

Unglued, like a snail
Being extracted,

From its shell.
Can I perform, my

*Experiment*
On you?

The horrible
Question, questions…

Point-blank, No!
I say, showing

*Vehemence!*
And walk away.

## Dreaming of Seville, Spain

I awoke, dreaming
About a life, I
Had lived, in Seville,
Spain, in 1988—
Where I am watching
Myself, looking-out
Over, my landlord's
Terrace, on *Asuncion
Calle*, in view of
Expensive boutiques,
And a *Panaderia*
Around the corner—
Opposite, the cute
*Escuela*, I attended.
In the dream—
I bend down briskly,
Silencing the wind,
Shaking, the wet-clothes
Hanging, on a line
2 blocks, away.
The ground below
Cowers, covered by
Rickety copper-
Colored leaves, skating
Under, the blackened
Sky. Huge fish, gone
*Loco*, jump, like trick
Dolphins, from a murky
Pond, at the *Maria
Louisa Park*, catching
Soggy bread-bits, I threw
At them, until, the
Plastic-bag falls, limp.

Their mouths are so big—
Like, an inviting door
I could walk through—
And I imagine,
They could hear, the blood
Rushing from my head,
As I rise, from the bed
Startled, after a
Fishy-eyeball, glitters
Into my face, like
A mirror, I cannot
Begin to escape.

## The Healing

It disappeared.
The red, sandy
beach, vanished, as
love, had finished
its cycle, of
healing, the beats,
of the romantic
hearts, by depositing
its passion—a real
existence, in their
minds, for all of
eternity—
finding, a place,
to hide its heat—
its mystery,
in those, who captured
and played, with it—
now, received, a
healing, gift, deep
within, the universe—
so, unable, to
close, its doors—
making, life small.
I watched, the full
enticing, moon,
channel thoughts, to
my mind, as if
the *Gods*, were proud
of their great
existence, so
within, their new
creations, for

*tonight*, speaking
to all, who pondered
the question: Who am
I, deep within, this
bright, starry, universe,
so intelligent?
The answers became
more, substantial
and capable, of
being enjoyed
By those, who received
The gift—channeled
Only, to those, who
Questioned, their potential
For divine, goodness.

**Save the Good Children**

> *Some 805 million people in the world do not have enough food to lead a healthy active life. That's about one in nine people on earth.*
> —World Food Programme

Have you ever *Preyed*
With a bird, hoping
To find food, before
He does? Try competing
With nature's wildlife
For your survival!
*Save the good children!*

Your stomach is bloated
With worms, as your
Gaunt arms, and elbows
Grovel, in the
Barren, disease-
Infested earth.
*Save the good children!*

Your head is bowed
In humiliation,
And together
You, and the
Despondent bird
*Pray*, for another
Day, and hour
Until, there is, a
Chance for survival.
*Save the good children!*

## Grandma Rhodes Remembered from a Photo Taken in Florida

At age 8, I vacationed
In Key Biscayne. A photo
Remains, of Grandma Rhodes, with
A big straw hat on, posing
On the opal, sandy

Crescent beach, smiling, as I
Stood, with her warm arms, hugging
My shoulders. I beam under
The sun, sun-tanned. My long brown
Wavy hairdo, with bangs, blows
From the sea bursting, and I
Am Safe, inside, my wraparound
Yellow print skirt, and white blouse.
The sand glistens, like cat's eyes—
Mysterious, and God-like,
As the blue waves, rock and roll
Generously, onto, shore.
Gentle youth, waved its sweet tongue
At me, saying: *Cherish these
Breaths—a Mother, Father, Sister
Paternal Grandmother...always.*

During Easter, Grandma's reddened
Hand, burned from the raw, hot sun,
Clutching palm leaves, and her ring
Finger, swollen from age, bulged
Underneath a copper ring—
Supposed to heal arthritis.
Her hands were veiny, and red
Like my hands, are veiny now.
I felt we shared, a strong bond
Even, after her death, at

92-years-old. As a
Devout Catholic, she prayed each
Day, with her *Rosary* beads
Each morning, at 6 am
In a soft, meditative
Whisper. Each finger, careful
To rub a bead, in memory
Of someone who passed, or for her
Family, or others, in need.
I remember, the sweet scent
In her room: a mixture of
*Cashmere Bouquet* talcum powder,
*Milk of Magnesia* tablets,
Assorted candies, and the
Strange odor, of canary
Food conditioner. My best
Pastime, was watching Grandma's
Canary, Mimi, nibble
Heartily, at a rope of bird
Seed, and listening to the
Nurturing sounds, of her beak
Scratching, at her cuttlebone,
Before pecking at her breakfast
Of scrambled eggs. Mimi talked
In the morn, and I would knock
On Grandma's door, before peeking
In, and once welcomed inside,
I would sit on her bed, and
Listen, to Mimi, *mimic* her:
"I'm mama's little baby."
"I'm mama's little baby."

My sharp-witted, blue-eyed Grandma,
Was a *Fabulous*, storyteller.
I remember the story, of
The little boy, who vomited
Snakes, out of his throat. This story
Was told, to warn me, about
What happened, to children, who
Were disobedient. Other
Stories, she told were about, the
Horrid, lice-infestations
That took place, in school, and how
She had to get, her long, waist-
Length hair, chopped off, to rid her
Of those pesky-parasites.
Grandma suffered prejudice
Too, in grammar school, when her
White teacher, threw all her prized
Rings, into the garbage, for
Punishment, but her German Step-
Father, soon intervened, scolding
Her teacher, good! She said, he was

A great, Step-Dad, and really
Loved him. Her real father, was an
Irishman, and drove a *Rolls Royce*.
And later, when she married
He came to visit her. He liked
All her children, and offered them
Various jobs, and equipment
For the movie, projector
Business, but none were ambitious.
Soon, Grandma's spouse, died, from TB—

The second tragedy, after
Her first son, died, from pneumonia
Days, after, he was just born.
And so, she began, working at
The police-station, making
Beds, because, her husband's, small
Police pension, was not enough
Money, to make ends meet. So all
The male children, dropped out of school
And got jobs, to help support, the
Family. She raised her 6 children

And kneaded them, the way, she made
Bread. Some weekends, she visited
Her youngest, son's home—(my father's
House), her favorite child, and baked
Hot rolls, so sweet—butter churned
And fluffy, yellow inside—
Better than Jewish Challah bread!
The aroma, awakened
The morning sun, spreading its
Sticky fingers, on the warm
Kitchen window. A glass table
With green legs, captured the light
Drawing, it into our breakfast
Plates, warming the food, nourishing
Our bodies, and hearts and souls.

**Unspoken Butterflies**

Butterflies, with yellow, and black wings
Hang, on purple patches, seeking songs
Of unspoken words, attracting my silky
Whispers, to speak stories aloud, but
Not from afar: "Butterflies, butterflies
Are yellow and black, wings crimsoned in
Purple, sending unspoken words!"

## I'd Like To

I'd like to go shopping, and walk right
Into the A&P, and sift, through loose
Candy, loaded in the bins, of the tasty
Produce department. I'd like to sample
All the different flavors, of ice cream,
*Rum Raisin* especially, and get drunk
Off its aroma. I'd like to eat a hunky
Piece, of thick, Swedish, dark chocolate
And fill my house, with bricks of it—
Housing myself inside, its sweet cocoa
Aroma—and still feel skinny. I'd like to
Fill my ribs with tofu (sausages, hotdogs,
Bologna) sandwiches and to imagine
What it's like to *never* feel hungry.
I'd like to brag and boast, about what a
Great shape I have, as I wear my dreamy
20-year old, yellow, with a small heart
Cut out, in the back of the Bikini
Bottom, while bronzing on the hot beach.
I'd like to peel back, the layers of tight
Skin, to when I was 12 or 13,
—And admire myself through the eyes
Of *Zeus*, (the sun god). I'd like to baste
In the sun, until the sheer light, shadowed
Me, into the grey mist, of sunset.

## Congelese Confidence
### *(for M'Sevumba)*

What opportunities can I create? I'm
A widow, abandoned by my husband's
Brother, but I'm beautiful and rare, and I
Care, for my 10 children. I live, in the *Nation
Of Congo*, where roads are dirt paths, jut with sharp
Rocks. I wear, what I have: wobbly flip-flops. I
Can feel, each grain nub, of the land, as I walk—
As I predict, the density, of each hill's slope,
Sculpted, into the strong arch, and sinew core
Of my feet. Steady with stealth, of a lion-
Ness; I maneuver my load, across the land.
I'm a *Congolese Mother*, and I'm proud! I
Walk across, thin wood beams, over swampy water—
The only way, to reach my destination
In the *big city*. I'm like a tightrope walker,
Imagining, my great destiny. I don't
Dare, look back! I'm also a magician
With a heavy load, that lifts, like the wind, *sweet-talks*
My back. I'll be your *porter*—I'll carry your
Bed—your 100-pound, bag of grain, for only
25-cents. Why? Because, I'm a *Congolese
Mother*, and I'm proud! I will never, balk—
I have too much dignity, and mighty esteem
Emanates, from the roots, of my nerve fibers.
*God*, has answered my prayer command!

**Self-Love**

Sometimes, each laugh, feels
Luminous, over virtuous ears.
Early, little, fine lines—oh vanity
Evaporates!
Laugh's fuzzy, leaden, old-fashioned
Visitor's eye—
Fairest livelong, of very earth—
Lightening, one-velvet ear,
On veil effacing—
Visited early,
Eternity!

When **Lisa Rhodes-Ryabchich** left the Army as an E4 in 1992, she had only a vague notion that she wanted to be a writer but after finding some of her mother's poems, she convinced herself that she too must have great metaphoric talent and began to take Dan Masterson's and Suzanne Cleary's poetry workshops at Rockland Community College in Suffern, N.Y. After she mastered those classes, she applied at Sarah Lawrence College in Bronxville, N.Y. and after 2 rejections, she joined their MFA poetry-writing program and graduated in 1999. Her mentor was Tom Lux and he was a marvelous teacher and very kind and caring. She was an enthusiastic student who interviewed Maxine Kumin over the phone for the "Phoenix" school newspaper. She had admired Anne Sexton and so just talking with Maxine was exciting. After graduating, she published some poems, worked as a life insurance agent, cashier at Pathmark (the 10pm-2am shift), substitute teacher and finally as an English Adjunct at Ramapo College and Bergen Community College before falling in love and getting married to a Russian Air Force Veteran in 2003. Her marriage ended tragically after her child got sick and finding out that her husband was unfit for marriage and raising a special-needs child. Luckily, her ability to turn lemons into lemonade enabled her to stay strong and persevere. After taking a few workshops through Cave Canem in NYC, she realized it was her or nobody that was going to make-it. She began to write more seriously and resurrected her poems from the forgotten files and started editing. Her hard work paid off and her first chapbook "We Are beautiful Like Snowflakes" was accepted for publication by http://www.finishinglinepress.com. She was glorified! Her most recent poems (The Goddess poems) were born after listening to the poet Gregory Pardlo who uses such great imagery and lots of imagination. Presently, she plans on finishing this series, which empowers women and sends a message of healing and grace.

Furthermore, she is a strong self-determined single-mom of a 12-year old 100-pound lovable child named Kyla. Kyla is her only daughter, born when she turned 40 years old. Her daughter has a disabling condition called quadriplegia, cerebral palsy, and epilepsy. She was her miracle child who survived strep B meningitis, which she contracted at 6 weeks of age after being born at 36 weeks. Her child has beaten the odds and survived a horrible illness. Her child is non-verbal but can use yes/no signs when prompted. She has a beautiful smile and a great spirit. Lisa has thanked God her child has receptive skills and understands what she says to her otherwise she would not feel that halo of love after complimenting her and get to see her pearly white teeth and dimples flash. Throughout her 12-year journey with her daughter she has written articles as well as numerous poems about her daughter's illnesses. Her poetry manuscript about her daughter's fight with strep B meningitis is entitled "The Fight To Live: Poems From Surviving Strep B Meningitis & Epilepsy" and is presently seeking a publisher. Her daughter, Kyla has been a huge advocate and inspiration for her writing. Her daughter's little face lights up when she reads her the poems and she feels urged on to write after seeing her daughter's gleeful enthusiasm. She knows her daughter wants her to be successful because she feels her daughter takes pride in her many accomplishments because after all her daughter has helped to implement them.

Additionally, Lisa has a B.A. in Communications from St. Thomas Aquinas College in Sparkill, N.Y., a Computer Science Certificate in Business Applications from SUNY Purchase in Purchase, N.Y., a B.S. in Journalism from Mercy College in Dobbs Ferry, N.Y., a Television News Production Certificate from New York University in Manhattan, N.Y., and a B.A. in Speech Pathology and Audiology from Lehman College in the Bronx, N.Y.

Furthermore, Lisa has been a mentor for Pen Americas Prison Writing Program, which helps prisoners reach their literary potential, promotes healing and rehabilitation.

Finally, some of her poems have been published by and can be seen at http://www.praxismagonline.com, www.youblisher.com/pdf/884760, Obsidian III, Journal of Poetry Therapy, Footsteps, AIM, Left Jab, Poetry Motel, poemhunter.com, Peaceful Poetry to Love Your Societal Consciousness, and elsewhere.

Her published articles are:
1. Rhodes, L. (2011) Poetry Writing as a Healing Method in Coping with a Special Needs Child: A Narrative Perspective. Journal of Poetry Therapy: The Interdisciplinary Journal of Practice, Theory, Research and Education, v 24, n 2 p.117-125 Sum
2. Rhodes, L. (2002) Poetry and a Prison Writing Program: A Mentor's Narrative Report. Journal of Poetry Therapy, v15 n3 p163-68 Spr

www.ingramcontent.com/pod-product-compliance
Lightning Source LLC
LaVergne TN
LVHW041505070426
835507LV00012B/1330